ACCESSING THE
COURTS OF
HEAVEN

DESTINY IMAGE BOOKS
BY ROBERT HENDERSON

*Unlocking Destinies from the
Courts of Heaven Curriculum*

Unlocking Destinies from the Courts of Heaven

Operating in the Courts of Heaven

ACCESSING THE

COURTS OF HEAVEN

HOW TO POSITION YOURSELF FOR
BREAKTHROUGH IN PRAYER

ROBERT HENDERSON

DESTINY IMAGE® PUBLISHERS, INC.

P.O. Box 310, Shippensburg, PA 17257-0310

"Promoting Inspired Lives."

This book and all other Destiny Image and Destiny Image Fiction books are available at Christian bookstores and distributors worldwide.

Cover design by Eileen Rockwell

Interior design by Terry Clifton

For more information on foreign distributors, call 717-532-3040.

Reach us on the Internet: www.destinyimage.com.

ISBN 13 TP: 978-0-7684-1740-1

ISBN 13 eBook: 978-0-7684-1741-8

For Worldwide Distribution, Printed in the U.S.A.

2 3 4 5 6 7 8 / 21 20 19 18 17

CONTENTS

Part One

THE COURTS OF HEAVEN PRAYER STRATEGY

Chapter 1

THREE DIMENSIONS OF PRAYER

We have a little dog named Otis. Otis is about 14 pounds with long, shaggy hair. His mother is a dachshund mixed with terrier or poodle or something else. That's just who Otis is, and we love the little guy.

One day our six-year-old grandson, Jackson, was in the living room with Otis, and he doesn't know anybody's around. My wife sees Jackson on the floor with Otis. Jackson is gently holding Otis's head in his hands and looking into his eyes. Jackson says to Otis, "Otis, if you want to be a super-hero, you're going to have to change the way you think. The first thing you have to do is get a cape. The second thing you need is a superhero name like Super Dog. And the third thing you need to do is learn how to fly."

If we want to move in the supernatural, we have to change the way we think.

I tell people that my grandson understands more than we do about how the Kingdom of God operates. If we want to move in the supernatural, we have to change the way we think.

Our natural way of thinking does not lend itself to moving into the supernatural realms—and the Courts of Heaven are in the supernatural realm of God.

THREE DIMENSIONS OF PRAYER

Jesus put prayer in three different dimensions—*Father, Friend, Judge.* The first dimension of approaching God as Father is found in Luke 11 and 18. The Holy Spirit reveals the fatherhood of God, heals our wounds, comforts us, etc. We fall in love with the Father and come into greater revelation of how deeply the Father loves us. Jesus says, *"When you pray, say: Our Father in heaven"* (Luke 11:2). So, the first dimension of prayer is approaching God as Father.

In Luke 11:5-6 (NIV), Jesus says, *"Suppose you have a friend, and you go to him at midnight and say, 'Friend, lend me three loaves of bread; a friend of mine on a journey has come to me, and I have no food to offer him."* The second dimension of prayer is approaching God as Friend.

Jesus was teaching the disciples the three dimensions of prayer. The first one related to God as Father, which is about getting our own needs and desires met. The second realm is approaching God as Friend, with the picture Jesus painted of a man who had a friend in need and couldn't help him, so he went to another friend. We are the ones who can't help, but we can go to our Friend for help—we are in a position of intercession.

> *We come before God the Father
> for our own needs and desires.
> We come before God as Friend for
> the needs of others. But we come
> before God as Judge when we're
> dealing with an adversary.*

In Luke 18:1-8, Jesus teaches on prayer through a parable, showing the disciples that they should always pray and not give up. He tells them there was a widow who came before an unjust judge and wanted justice from her adversary. He didn't agree right away, but he finally gave her what she wanted because she kept nagging him. Jesus told them that God will quickly avenge His own elect who cry out day and night to Him.

The third dimension of prayer is that of approaching the Judge or going into a judicial system. When

Jesus spoke of a widow approaching an unjust judge, He was not saying God is an unjust judge; He was saying that if a widow could get a verdict from an unjust judge, how much *more* can we, His children, come before the righteous Judge, the Judge of all the earth, and see Him render verdicts on our behalf and in our favor.

We come before God the Father for our own needs and desires. We come before God as Friend for the needs of others. But we come before God as Judge when we're dealing with an adversary.

Chapter 2

BREAKTHROUGH IN THE
COURT OF HEAVEN

We must realize that prayer is a conflict. Have you ever felt conflict in prayer? Maybe you're praying and you're thinking, *I don't understand why I'm feeling this way. I'm not sure why I'm sending this prayer to God and there seems to be a conflict.* The conflict you're in is not a battlefield; it is actually a judicial system or a courtroom.

Courtrooms are places of conflict, and we are dealing with an adversary seeking to prevent God's will from being done in our lives. The Bible says in First Peter 5:8 that we should *"Be sober, be vigilant; because your adversary the devil walks about like a roaring lion, seeking whom he may devour."* The word for "adversary" in First Peter 5:8 and in Luke 18 is the same word—the Greek word *antidikos,* which means one who brings a lawsuit. It's a legal position.

The conflict you're in is not a battlefield; it is actually a judicial system or a courtroom.

BREAKTHROUGHS

If we're going to get breakthrough in the midst of the conflict, we have to understand what the conflict is. It's in the legal system or the judicial systems of the spirit realm, and we have to know how to come before God, not just as Father, not just as Friend, but also as Judge and deal with the adversaries and the issues that are attacking us.

Many people have been praying for a long time but haven't had any breakthrough. God wants to bring breakthrough to us, but we have to know how to go into the third dimension of prayer. Let's look at Revelation 12:10-12, which brings additional insight:

> *Then I heard a loud voice saying in heaven, "Now **salvation, and strength, and the kingdom of our God, and the power of His Christ have come**, for the **accuser** of*

our brethren, who accused them before our God day and night, **has been cast down**. *And they overcame him by the blood of the Lamb and by the word of their testimony, and they did not love their lives to the death. Therefore rejoice, O heavens, and you who dwell in them! Woe to the inhabitants of the earth and the sea! For the devil has come down to you, having great wrath, because he knows that he has a short time."*

Has there been a full manifestation of the Kingdom of God on earth? No. If the Kingdom was fully manifest, the moment people got saved they would be instantly healed, delivered, and made completely whole in the here and now. If the Kingdom was fully manifest, cities would be reformed and nations would be discipled.

We have not yet seen a full manifestation of the Kingdom as we would understand it today. So obviously when John says *"have come,"* he wasn't talking about the present "now" or even the "now then"; he was speaking of something that was yet to come. He was hearing the sound of something that was yet to materialize, yet to be manifest, because we're still pressing and pushing for a full manifestation of the Kingdom. If there is a full manifestation of the Kingdom, every realm of breakthrough you've been desiring, you now have.

John continues, *"For the accuser of our brethren, who accused them before our God day and night, has been cast down."* Here, he explains the reason a full manifestation of the Kingdom had come was because there was no longer an accuser able to speak against us. This word for "accuser" is the Greek word *kategoros,* and it means a complainant in a legal system—a plaintiff at law.

If we want our full breakthrough, we have to deal with the accuser, the one preventing us from getting what God wants us to have.

It's someone who is bringing a complaint against you in the judicial system of Heaven. That's why it says the accuser, or this *kategoros,* is complaining or bringing a case against us in the Courts of Heaven—and his complaint against us stops our full breakthrough. John wrote that the full breakthrough comes when the accuser is silenced, when he's fully dealt with. If he's not fully dealt with and he still has a case against us, then the result is that we have not yet experienced our full breakthrough.

If we want our full breakthrough, we have to deal with the accuser, the one preventing us from getting what God wants us to have. Remember, First Peter 5:8 says that the *antidikos* is the one who brings a lawsuit. The same idea, a different word. *Antidikos* comes from two words—*anti*, which means to deny, and *dikos*, which means right. Our adversary, the devil, is using his accusations against us to deny us what's rightfully ours. Jesus died for us to have everything. Then why don't we have it? Because there is still a case against us that needs to be dealt with!

There is still a case against us in the spirit realm—it's that simple. We haven't experienced the full manifestation of the Kingdom yet, not because we haven't won the victory on the battlefield; rather, it's because we've yet to get the case answered in the courtroom of Heaven. This is functioning in the third dimension of prayer.

You have been praying for breakthrough but haven't seen any results because there's still an accusation against you in the spirit realm. The lack of breakthrough is not because of timing. "Oh, I'm just waiting on God to answer me, and it's about to kill me while I'm waiting. *I'm just waiting on the timing of God.*" Meanwhile, everything is falling to pieces around us—there's divorce and financial ruin and people dying prematurely, but we're "waiting on God." That's not the God I serve.

It's not a timing issue; it's a legal issue. If we can get the legal issue dealt with, if we can get the case answered, and if we can get the accuser silenced, then we can have our breakthrough by moving into the third realm of prayer.

Part Two

THREE KEYS
TO UNLOCK
BREAKTHROUGH
IN THE COURTS
OF HEAVEN

In this next section, I want to share three keys that, when understood and applied, will give you access to breakthrough and answer prayer in the Courts of Heaven.

The three keys you need to apply in order to step into the third dimension of prayer and answer the case against you in the Courts of Heaven are based on Revelation 12:11.

> *And they overcame him by the blood of the Lamb and by the word of their testimony, and they did not love their lives to the death.*

1. The blood of the Lamb

2. The word of your testimony

3. Not loving your life until death

When we walk in the third dimension of prayer, we are able to answer any and every accusation against us that the adversary would use to stop the full breakthrough that we desire from coming into our lives.

The enemy has spent a long time building a case against you. If someone files a suit against you, they have evidence against you and have spent time putting this case together. The enemy is the same way.

Satan has spent a long time putting together cases against us because he doesn't want us coming into the full breakthrough God has for us. But Jesus, by what He has done on the cross, has given us everything we need to answer every case, silence the accuser, and see the fullness of what God wants for us to become reality in our lives. This ought to raise the level of our excitement and expectation when it comes to the place of prayer.

In the next three chapters, I want us to study each of those three keys separately, beginning with the *blood of the Lamb*.

Chapter 3

THE BLOOD THAT SPEAKS

*And they overcame him by
the blood of the Lamb.*
—REVELATION 12:11

When you sit in a natural courtroom, you hear a variety of voices—witnesses, jurors, the judge, bailiffs, etc. There are voices in the Courts of Heaven as well, and eight of those are mentioned in Hebrews 12:22-24. In the spiritual dimension of the Courts, the last thing mentioned is *"the blood that speaks better things than that of Abel."*

In Genesis 4:9 when Cain kills Abel, God comes to Cain and says, *"Where is Abel your brother?"* Cain says *"I do not know. Am I my brother's keeper?"* God replies, *"What have you done? The voice of your brother's blood cries out to Me from the ground. ...A fugitive and a vagabond you shall be on the earth"* (Gen. 4:9-10,12b).

When the Bible says we overcome the accuser by the blood, it is because we come into agreement with what the blood is saying. The blood gives God the legal right to forgive.

On the basis of the testimony of Abel's blood, God judged and sentenced Cain. The blood has spoken (past tense) but it also speaks (present tense). It is still speaking (see Heb. 12:24). Jesus' blood speaks to us even today.

SIX THINGS THE BLOOD OF JESUS IS SPEAKING

1. The blood of Jesus prophesies: it actively speaks.

   The blood is prophetic in nature. The blood that has spoken may not be prophetic. But when the blood is still speaking, that means it has a prophetic element connected to it, and we can pick up in the spirit what the blood is saying. This is the whole dimension of Hebrews 12:22-24 — the prophetic dimension — where we can begin to discern and understand.

2. The blood of Jesus speaks forgiveness: it gives God the legal right to forgive sins.

When the Bible says we overcome the accuser by the blood, it is because we come into agreement with what the blood is saying. Now thank God that whenever I sin or any realm that I fail in, I can say, "Lord, I'm asking for Your blood to speak for me. I thank You that Your blood is speaking for me, and I'm asking that this sin (fault or whatever it may be) be covered with the blood of Jesus. I'm asking for the blood to speak." What does the blood do? The blood gives God the legal right to forgive.

How do I know this? When the priests in the Old Testament went behind the veil once a year on the Day of Atonement, they would sprinkle the blood of the Passover lamb, and the testimony of that blood administered by the High Priest granted God the legal right to remove the sins from the people of Israel for one more year. That's what the blood did.

3. *The blood of Jesus testifies in the court of Heaven*: the

blood of Jesus, our High Priest, gives God the legal right to pardon sin forever.

The good news is that under the new and better covenant, we have a High Priest after the Order of Melchizedek. His name is Jesus (see Heb. 7:17). He has taken His own blood and poured it out on our behalf. He has sprinkled it, and His blood is speaking as a testimony before the Courts of Heaven. It is giving God the legal right to not only remove our sins but to totally forgive our sins forever. That's what the blood is doing. It's a legal element speaking on our behalf.

> *Every accusation that the enemy would bring against you in the court of Heaven, you have the right to answer by the blood.*

4. *The blood of Jesus testifies against the accusations of satan*: the redemptive work of Jesus answers every accusation the devil would bring against you.

You have to know what the blood is doing if you're going to overcome by the blood. Every accusation that the enemy would bring against you in the court of Heaven, you have the right to answer by the blood. I want you to know there's not one accusation the devil can bring that the blood can't answer. The blood of Jesus can answer any and every accusation.

5. *The blood of Jesus speaks of Jesus' faithful and legal nature.* For the blood to answer our accusation, we have to repent.

First John 1:9 clearly says, *"If we confess our sins, He is faithful and just to forgive us our sins and to cleanse us from all unrighteousness."* Notice the legal language. "Faithful" speaks to His covenant-keeping nature. "Just" speaks to His legal nature. He's faithful and just to forgive. When we confess our sins, we are activating the legal realm that God operates in so the blood can speak on our behalf and God has the legal right to forgive us. We overcome by the blood of Jesus—the blood deals with all our failures.

6. The blood of Jesus speaks of Jesus' passion for the people of God to win for the Lamb the rewards of His suffering.

Jesus' blood is crying out for everything He spilled it for to become a reality. You see, the blood doesn't just forgive. The blood doesn't just protect. The blood of Jesus cries out for His purpose to be done on the earth. This is where we

have to have an ear to pro-
phetically hear what the
blood is speaking. When
you start picking up what
the blood is saying, it will
stir the passion of God
inside you. You will then
begin to agree with the dec-
larations of His blood and
you say, "Lord, everything
You laid Your life down
for, let it become a reality in
my life and in the world."

*Jesus' blood is crying out
for everything He spilled it
for to become a reality.*

God wants to bring that spirit into
the Church again. The Moravians,
organized in the 1400s, are known to
have prayed so much and had such

hearts to evangelize the world that they would sell themselves into slavery so they could go to foreign lands and tell people about Jesus whom they would not have otherwise had an opportunity to tell. It's said that as they were loaded onto ships for destinations unknown, they would sing, "that we might win for the Lamb the rewards of His suffering, that the passion of our heart is to lay our lives down and win for the Lamb the *rewards* of His suffering."

> *If we're going to silence the accuser, we have to agree with the blood and what it's speaking.*

That's why we are here on earth. Sometimes we mistakenly think we're here just to get blessed. God does *not* want to simply bless us. Yes, He loves us deeply and wants to express that love in the form of blessing. However, we're also here to lay down our lives so everything Jesus died for becomes a reality. His blood, the message, and what the blood is saying is also about His passion being fulfilled on the earth. If we're going to silence the accuser, we have to agree with the blood and what it's speaking.

Let's pray together:

> *Lord, I want You to know that I agree with Your blood. I agree that Your blood brings healing, salvation, forgiveness, and protection. I agree that the blood causes You to remember me.*

> *Lord, I agree with Your blood and I thank You for the blood of Jesus. Lord Jesus, I thank You for the blood that You shed for*

*me. I don't take it for granted. I
know how precious it is. Thank
You, Lord!*

Chapter 4

THE WORD OF TESTIMONY

And they overcame him…by the word of their testimony.
—REVELATION 12:11

The second thing John writes: *"and they overcame him…by the word of their testimony."* The word *testimony* means those who give judicial witness. It's a legal term. We overcome the enemy by the word of our testimony. There are many different things in the spirit realm that are received in the Courts of Heaven as testimony. We need to make sure that our words are in agreement with God's passion. And we need to make sure our prophetic words are in agreement with His passion.

DRY BONES OR A MIGHTY ARMY?

For instance, in Ezekiel 37:1-14, Ezekiel is dropped down in the valley of dry bones. God says to him, *"Can these bones live?"* Ezekiel says, *"O Lord God, You know."* Why that response? Because he was struggling; in the natural, his eyes saw the valley of dry bones, but in the spirit he heard a marching army. Ezekiel had to choose whether to agree with his eyes—what he observed in the natural realm—or his ears—what he heard rumbling in the spirit. He chose to agree with what his ears heard and he began to prophesy. As Ezekiel released testimony in the Courts, this allowed the bones to come together, flesh and sinew wrapped around them, and the breath of God entered them so that they stood up on their feet as a mighty army. All of this was based on what Ezekiel chose to prophesy.

It's really easy to look at the natural state of things and prophesy wrong things. This is simply agreeing with the situation or circumstance *as is*. Then, when what was prophesied happens, the person says, "I told you that was God." No, it didn't happen because it was God; it happened because it was prophesied and released as testimony in the Courts of Heaven. That's what people don't get. *How can this be?* they ask. Let's look at a story in the Bible that helps illustrate this further.

Ezekiel had to choose whether to agree with his eyes — what he observed in the natural realm — or his ears — what he heard rumbling in the spirit.

WHAT TESTIMONY ARE YOU PROPHESYING?

Twelve spies went into Canaan and when they returned ten of them gave an evil report—a bad testimony (see Num. 13:32). What did God do? He rendered a verdict against the nation because ten of the spies gave the wrong testimony. Because of those ten spies—recognized as a government in the Courts of Heaven where they gave the wrong testimony—God basically said, "On the basis of your testimony, I have no alternative. I render a judgment: you'll wander in the wilderness for forty years." It's shocking, but true—ten people determined the destiny of a nation for forty years.

We'd better be careful what we prophesy. I'm upset with all the doomsday prophets today. I'd like to tell each of them, "Please be quiet. Please don't say that. Please don't prophesy that. Prophesy what's in the books of Heaven about a nation. Prophesy the good word of the Lord, what God has actually intended—not what you see in the natural." We need people who can prophesy what the Spirit of God is saying and see the good even in the midst of the bad and see the intent of

God. I love that, because those are the ones releasing testimonies that will bring breakthroughs and positive verdicts from God. We overcome by the word of our testimony.

We need people who can prophesy as to what the Spirit of God is saying and see the good even in the midst of the bad and see the intent of God.

SHARING FINANCES RELEASES THE POWER OF TESTIMONY

We also release testimony when we share our financial resources with God's Kingdom on earth. Hebrews 7:8 says, *"Here mortal men receive tithes, but there he receives them, of whom it is witnessed that he lives."* Every time we give an offering, we are releasing the testimony. The writer of Hebrews is talking about us transitioning from the Levitical priesthood to the Melchizedek priesthood. The Levitical priesthood is about legalism. The Melchizedek priesthood is about honor. As we give our tithes under the Melchizedek order, we honor who Jesus is as our High Priest.

The word *witness* in Hebrews 7:8 means to give a judicial testimony. Every time you give your money, you're releasing a testimony. Whatever is in your heart when you give that tithe or offering is a testimony that speaks in the Courts of Heaven. This is *not* simply addressing giving to a local church or ministry, although that is certainly part of the case. Here, we are dealing with the very motive that compels giving in any capacity,

giving that is influenced by the Holy
Spirit living within you.

CONTENTION AND
STRIFE CREATES A
CASE AGAINST YOU

In Matthew 5:23-26, Jesus says:

> *Therefore if you bring your gift
> to the altar, and there remem-
> ber that your brother has some-
> thing against you, leave your
> gift there before the altar, and
> go your way. First be reconciled
> to your brother, and then come
> and offer your gift. Agree with
> your adversary quickly, while
> you are on the way with him,
> lest your adversary deliver you
> to the judge, the judge hand you
> over to the officer, and you be
> thrown into prison. Assuredly,*

I say that you, you will by no means get out of there till you have paid the very last penny.

If something is wrong between you and somebody else, there is a contention. There is a problem. You have bad feelings, which are often accompanied by ill will within. If this is the case, you must leave your gift at the altar and make things right. In other words, don't use the dispute as a reason not to give; use it as a reason to fix things so you can give freely. Jesus says to *leave your gift* at the altar, go be reconciled, and then come back to the altar and *offer your gift*.

Jesus says not to give your gift if there's a problem in your heart toward somebody else. Why would He say that? Verse 25 says, *"Agree with your adversary quickly, while you are on the way with him, lest your adversary deliver you to the judge, the judge hand you over to the officer, and you be thrown into prison. Assuredly, I say that you, you will by no means get out of there till you have paid the very last penny."* The reason you should not give your offering when you've got a problem in your heart is because your offering is releasing a testimony before the Judge, and the adversary can use it against you.

Every way we release testimony in the Courts of Heaven is designed to help us release a case that grants God the right to render verdicts in our behalf.

If you are offering your gift while harboring ill will toward others, your money is releasing the wrong testimony in the Courts of Heaven. I'll share a secret with you that will help unlock new levels of freedom and breakthrough—particularly in the financial realm. If you've given finances to the church and yet you have ongoing bitterness toward someone, you need to ask, "Lord, please let the testimony of those finances be annulled so that they can no longer speak against me. I know now that money is speaking in the Courts of Heaven, releasing a testimony that is empowering the accuser to bring the case against me." Money is very spiritual, so you need to set things right with God.

Again, this is not a reason to give or not give. This is a reason to get our hearts right so we can give and make the most impact for the Kingdom. If your offering is that powerful in the negative, how powerful is it in the positive? Every way we release testimony in the Courts of Heaven is designed to help us release a case that grants God the right to render verdicts in our behalf; we overcome by the blood but also the word of our testimony.

BRING AN OFFERING IN RIGHTEOUSNESS

Malachi 3:2-3 says:

> But who can endure the day of His coming? And who can stand when He appears? For He is like a refiner's fire and like launderers' soap. He will sit as a refiner and a purifier of silver; He will purify the sons of Levi, and purge them as gold and silver, that they may **offer**

to the Lord an offering in righteousness.

Why is God purifying us? So we can be holy? No. It's so we can bring an offering in righteousness. The whole reason for this purifying process is not so we can be holy, it is so we can bring an offering in righteousness. Our offerings are so powerful because they contain testimony. The Lord is taking us through a purifying process so that our hearts are right and pure.

We should not try to manipulate God with our money. Rather, we are bringing our finances to Him through His Church because we are declaring His worth and how much we love Him and how much our faith is in Him. That's what resonates in the Courts of Heaven. We can't think,

Well, I better give this, because if I don't, He might be mad at me. No, that's a wrong motive to give. That's trying to manipulate God.

THE TWO BLESSINGS OF BRINGING AN OFFERING IN RIGHTEOUSNESS

Malachi 3:4-5 says that two things will happen when we give an offering in righteousness:

> *"Then the offering of Judah and Jerusalem will be pleasant to the Lord, as in the days of old, as in former years. And I will come near you for judgment; I will be a swift witness against sorcerers, against adulterers, against perjurers, against those who exploit wage earners and widows and orphans, and*

> *against those who turn away an*
> *alien — because they do not fear*
> *Me," says the Lord of hosts.*

1. Offerings Made in Righteousness Release Societal Blessings (Large Scale)

God says our money releases a testimony and it will be pleasant, because we've allowed Him to purify our hearts, so that we give out of right, pure motives. Consider what the Lord says — our testimony actually empowers Him to release judgments from His Courts against every ill that afflicts society. It works on both the personal level *and* the macro level. God says when His ecclesia brings Him an offering in righteousness, He can judge adultery in society, the breakdown of marriage. He judges witchcraft and perjurers. He judges oppressive economic systems and sets society in order because His government, the Church, has brought Him offerings in righteousness with the right testimonies attached. That's how powerful it is. After realizing all of this truth, offering time at church means a whole lot more. You're in the Courts of Heaven when you bring an offering to the altar. That's on a big scale.

2. Offerings Made in Righteousness Release Personal Breakthrough (Personal Level)

Your offerings, presented in righteousness, are also making a difference on a personal level. Maybe you're fighting for your marriage—bring an offering in righteousness. Let that testimony speak in the Courts. Maybe there are people lying about you; bring an offering. Maybe you are not making enough money; bring an offering. Each time you bring an offering, you're releasing testimony because you're allowing God to purify your heart. As you bring your offerings in righteousness, the judicial hand of God is released to move on your behalf. This is overcoming obstacles by the word of your testimony.

In this dimension of prayer, you're not just asking the Father or even appealing to the Friend. You are bringing a case into the Courts of Heaven because that's what you do when you testify.

We need to break off any past offerings that were given in wrong ways because we didn't understand. I've had to do that. I didn't want to fall prey to some subtle motive of manipulation; I want to bring offerings in righteousness. We must allow Him to purify us so we can bring our offering in righteousness for Him to multiply our resources.

If in the past you have presented offerings and tithes with ungodly motives, I encourage you to pray:

> *Lord Jesus, if in any way I brought offerings to You with a wrong heart, with ill will, or with wrong motives, I'm asking, Lord, that any testimony that is yet lingering before Your courts connected to my offering—that's giving a testimony that allows the accuser to have a case against me—Lord, I ask for that testimony to be annulled by the blood of Jesus.*

Lord, I confess to You, out of ignorance or whatever, that I messed up, and I'm asking You to silence this offering and the words of the offering by Your blood. Lord, I want to bring my offerings to You because I love You, I worship You, I value You, and I'm moving in faith in You. I want my offering to speak from that realm, so I repent and I'm asking, Lord, for every word being used connected to past offerings to now be silenced, in Jesus' name.

Chapter 5

LAYING DOWN OUR LIVES

*And they did not love
their lives to the death.*
—REVELATION 12:11

To silence the accuser, we love not
our lives unto death. In other
words, we lay down our lives for
God. When we surrender our lives
to the Lord—to His purpose and His
will—that action carries great realms

of authority and influence in the Courts of Heaven. So we should make it a normal part of our prayer to say something such as, "Lord, not my will but Your will be done. I lay my life down before You."

When we surrender our lives to the Lord—to His purpose and His will—that action carries great realms of authority and influence in the Courts of Heaven.

THE ROLE OF RIGHTEOUSNESS IN THE COURTS OF HEAVEN

It is important to understand how significant righteousness is in the Courts of Heaven. In Ezekiel 14:14, God says that there was such judgment coming on Israel that even if Job, Samuel, and Noah were to intercede, only by their righteousness could they save themselves. They would not be able to change the verdict concerning Israel, nor would they even be able to save sons and daughters. They would only have enough righteousness to save themselves. This tells me that righteousness is very important in the Courts of Heaven—that our ability to present a case before the Courts of Heaven is connected to righteousness. If that's true, here is the issue—we can never be righteous enough on our own merits. We are made righteous "enough" only by who Jesus is and what He has done for us.

> *Walking in the light is not walking perfectly, it's walking honestly.*

The Bible says that Jesus became sin for us, so that we could become the righteousness of God. Even Isaiah 54:17 says that our righteousness is from Him. When I am walking in an open and honest relationship with Jesus, dealing with my stuff and my sin, then I have a right to stand before Him in righteousness. I can't say, "Well, I can live any way I want to and God will still deem me righteous." No, by faith we must follow Him, obey Him, seek Him. We must repent where we need to repent. Remember, First John 1:7 says that *"If we walk in the light as He is in the light, we have fellowship with one another, and the blood of Jesus Christ His Son cleanses us from all sin* [unrighteousness].*"* What does this mean? Walking in the light is not walking perfectly, it's walking honestly. It's being honest with God. I believe if our hearts and our attitudes are righteous, the Lord will deem us righteous because of the blood of His Son and of everything He accomplished.

Romans 4:3 says that *"Abraham believed God, and it was accounted to him for righteousness."* Abraham was deemed righteous because he heard the voice of God and believed God. Remember, faith has great power with God to cause us to be righteous. Romans 8:4 says that *"the righteous requirement of the law might be fulfilled in us who do not walk according to the flesh but according to the Spirit."* Because we in our flesh are weak, we must walk in righteousness by faith, believing what Jesus did; then out of the empowerment of the Spirit we obey whatever the Spirit tells us to do. Righteousness is never a result of keeping rules. Righteousness is the result of living

under the mandate and the governments of the Holy Spirit.

OBEDIENCE TO THE
HOLY SPIRIT

The Holy Spirit might say something is OK for you but not OK for me.
As believers, we are each held respon-
sible to live under the mandates of
the Spirit. The Lord has spoken to me
and told me there are things I cannot do, not because they're wrong but
because God wants me to obey Him.
These things have nothing to do with
right or wrong; they have everything
to do with direct obedience to Him in
the context of relationship. And so, I
seek to obey.

A few examples: God told Rees
Howells, the great intercessor, not
to wear a hat in public, which was

an insult and very out of the social order in his day. Back then, it was almost scandalous for men to be outside without wearing a hat. And yet, Howells said as long as he obeyed that mandate from God—which had nothing to do with right or wrong—he had what he called "a place of abiding," because he obeyed what the Spirit told him to do.

> *Righteousness is never a result of keeping rules. Righteousness is the result of living under the mandate and the governments of the Holy Spirit.*

William Seymour sat on Azusa Street in Los Angeles with a box over his head and prayed, and the glory would come. People would stop and visit him and tell him that he didn't need to sit with a box over his head. As soon as he took the box off, the glory stopped coming until he put the box back on his head. That makes no logical sense; it just has everything to do with obeying what the Spirit tells *you* to do.

Several times in my life God has given me points of obedience. As long as I'm walking in agreement, following what the Spirit is saying, I have a place of jurisdiction in the spirit realm to pray from that I might not have otherwise. It gives me another realm. Why? I am deemed righteous because I'm walking under the governments of the Spirit, not merely keeping rules and regulations. When we lay our lives down, we can operate in new realms that God wants us to move in. We must be willing to turn over our earthly lives for His use—for His glory.

In closing, let's pray to silence the accuser and present our cases before the Courts of Heaven with bold confidence so we can fulfill our destinies.

Make this prayer your own:

> *Lord, thank You! Thank You for the blood of the Lamb. Thank You that You teach me how to release the right testimony. I declare that I lay my life down out of the empowerment of the Spirit. This allows me, by the blood of Jesus, to stand in a place of righteousness where I am recognized in the Courts of Heaven.*
>
> *I can now present cases in the courts that bring breakthrough*

to me, to my family, and to every realm of jurisdiction that You have given me. Lord, I believe for great breakthrough in my personal life, in my home, my workplace, my church, my city, and my nation—yes, Lord, even the world. Thank You for that, in Jesus' name, amen!

YOUR NEXT STEPS IN THE COURTS OF HEAVEN

The basic principles outlined in this small book are precursors to *Operating in the Courts of Heaven* and all subsequent *Courts of Heaven* books.

I consider these teachings essential and preparatory for those who wish to engage in the *Courts of Heaven* strategy for seeing breakthrough in prayer.

Before you study the details of the *Courts of Heaven*—the Books in Heaven, the three dimensions of prayer, dissolving curses, retrieving books of destiny, etc.—I want you to have a solid foundation of what gives you a legal right to *enter into the courts* to begin with and receive breakthrough answers to prayer.

EXCLUSIVE PREVIEW OF
ROBERT HENDERSON'S
NEW BOOK—

*Receiving Healing from
the Courts of Heaven*

CHAPTER ONE

COMING IN EARLY 2018

THE COURTS OF HEAVEN AND HEALING

A minister friend of mine named Ray Austin who is a Methodist pastor was beset by tumors and bleeding on his pituitary gland. It came out of the blue with intense pain and trauma. The pain in his head was so intense that he could only sleep for 10 minutes at a time. The pain would then wake him up. This went on for an extended period of time. The doctors told him at first that this was the pain of a stage-four cancer victim even though the tumor was benign. They later adjusted their statement and told him this was the worst pain known to man. There was much prayer that was activated for him, yet the situation only worsened and there was no healing. Nothing the doctors did brought any relief. They had no ability to even manage the pain.

In the midst of this situation, I felt led to call Ray and pray with him over the phone. As I did, I experienced a tremendous burden of intercession. I began to lead Ray into the Courts of Heaven. We dealt with any sin, transgression, and iniquity that the devil could be using to bring this on Ray. By the way, if none of these are present and allowing the devil legal right, then we can just appeal to God as Father or even Friend. God's merciful and gracious heart will move in our behalf. But if there is legal ground the devil is working from, we must get it revoked and removed. In Ray's case, we especially zeroed in on anything in his ancestry where a covenant was made with any demonic power.

Ray is of African descent. As a result of this, we dealt with any covenant or agreement made with demonic gods by those in his history. We asked for the blood of the Lamb to annul these covenants. We requested that any place Ray's name and his family name was on an altar, that it be removed. As a good friend from Nigeria told me, "Every African understands altars." In African history, cities are dedicated to demonic entities. There is at least an altar in the spirit realm if not the natural that exist. On these altars are the names of the people in these cities that were dedicated to these demonic gods. The result is these gods claim these people and their bloodlines for themselves. They assert that this gives them the right to bring curses, sickness, tragedies, and troubles to them. This is why bad things can happen to good people. In the healing area, this is why people many times don't get permanently healed and well when prayed for. We sought to remove and have revoked any and every legal right of the devil to torment Ray with this sickness and disease. Ray experienced a measure of relief as we dealt with these legal issues before God's Court. Later that night the pain again woke Ray up. It probably had been around twelve hours since we prayed. As Ray got up in intense pain, he simply one more time began to pray and ask God to heal him. This time Ray laid down on the couch in his living room. The next thing he knew he heard his neighbors leaving for work. Ray realized he had been asleep for several hours, which he had not done in several weeks. Then he realized he had no pain. He checked things out for just a little while and then went into the bedroom where Jodie, his wife was sleeping. He awoke her and announced, "God has healed me!" He then explained what had happened. As the reality of what had been done began to impact them, they started crying, laughing, and rejoicing at the goodness of God. The goodness of God had manifested itself to them in an amazing way.

Here's the question. Why did the prayer of Ray in those early morning hours bring a result that all the other times had not? Did God suddenly decide He loved Ray? Did Ray and everyone else finally pray enough so God was convinced and would heal him? Or did something legal that the devil was using against Ray get revoked and removed so the heart of God toward him could be manifested? This is what I believe and so does Ray. When we dealt with in particular any covenantal right of the devil against Ray, God was free to heal Ray. Up until this time, the devil before the Courts of Heaven was demanding his rights to afflict Ray with this condition. Once the blood of Jesus removed these things, God's passion toward Ray could manifest. It wasn't enough to appeal to the Fatherhood of God or even the Friendship of Jesus. We needed to go before God as Judge and deal with the legal issue stopping the healing. Getting things legally in place in the spirit allowed God to answer Ray's prayer.

As I mentioned earlier, the devil can use sin, transgression, and iniquity as legal rights against our health and us. David spoke of these three words in Psalms chapter 32 and verses 1 through 3.

> *Blessed is he whose transgression is forgiven,*
> *Whose sin is covered.*
> *Blessed is the man to whom the Lord does not impute iniquity,*
> *And in whose spirit there is no deceit.*
> *When I kept silent, my bones grew old*
> *Through my groaning all the day long.*

Notice that David attributed his "bones growing old" to his refusal to deal with sin, transgression, and iniquity. "Bones growing old" is a reference to sickness and disease. But once David repented and experienced forgiveness, his body was restored. God was not afflicting David with sickness because of his sin. The devil was using this as a legal right to bring sickness against him. James chapter

1 and verses 13 and 17 tell us the nature and heart of God. Verse 13 says,

> *"Let no one say when he is tempted, "I am tempted by God"; for God cannot be tempted by evil, nor does He Himself tempt anyone."*

God does not use evil. It is against His very nature and person to do such a thing. Sickness is not of God. Again, sickness is the tool and oppression of the devil. James continues in verse 17 by declaring,

> *"Every good gift and every perfect gift is from above, and comes down from the Father of lights, with whom there is no variation or shadow of turning."*

God's nature is consistent and without variation. Only good and perfect gifts come from God. God is incapable of bringing evil, and this includes sickness. There is no darkness in Him. There isn't even a shadow.

When David spoke of his "bones growing old" because of his sin, transgression, or iniquity, he was not saying God was doing this. It was the devil taking advantage of David's present status in the spirit to bring this weakened physical condition. David's repentance took away the legal rights of the devil and allowed healing and restoration to come.

I have dealt with these issues of sin, transgression, and iniquity in my earlier books on *The Courts of Heaven*. Let's look at these though from the healing perspective. These are the three primary things the devil uses to build cases against us that allow sickness to attack us. Remember, the devil operates from a legal perspective. First Peter chapter 5 and verse 8 speaks of this position.

> *Be sober, be vigilant; because your adversary the devil walks about like a roaring lion, seeking whom he may devour.*

Again the word "adversary" is the Greek word "antidikos". This word means an opponent in a lawsuit. This word is made up of two words, "anti" and "dikos". "Anti" means instead of or in the place of. We also know "anti" means to be against. The word "dikos" means rights as self-evident. So the words together mean to "stand against rights", or "what is rightfully ours". The adversary is one who brings a lawsuit to take away and deny what is rightfully ours. This very clearly is the tactic of the devil. Healing is what belongs to us legally. We will see this in the next chapter. Suffice it to say for now that healing is the children's bread. Jesus spoke of this in Mark chapter 7 and verses 26 through 27. A Gentile woman came to Jesus desiring healing and deliverance for her daughter. Jesus denied her at first because she wasn't a Jew. The New Covenant had not yet been put into place by Jesus' work on the cross. The Old Covenant that was for the Jewish people alone was still in operation. As a result of this Jesus makes a profound statement about healing and deliverance.

> *The woman was a Greek, a Syro-Phoenician by birth, and she kept asking Him to cast the demon out of her daughter. But Jesus said to her, "Let the children be filled first, for it is not good to take the children's bread and throw it to the little dogs."*

Jesus calls healing "the children's bread." In other words, it is the covenant right of those who belong to God to be healed. If this was true under the Old Covenant, how much more under the New Covenant that is full of better promises. (Heb. 8:6) Even though healing is ours as New Testament believers, we still see those who are not being healed. The reason for this is the devil has built a case against us as the adversary or antidikos that is denying us what is rightfully ours. We must know how to deal with him from the legal dimension of the spirit. This means we must approach God as Judge in His judicial system of Heaven and undo every case against us. Before we can do this however, we must know what he uses to build those cases and deny our healing!

There is one more portion of Scripture we need to investigate to understand the devil's legal maneuvering in the spirit realm. Revelation chapter 12 and verses 10 and 11 shows this to us.

> *Then I heard a loud voice saying in heaven, "Now salvation, and strength, and the kingdom of our God, and the power of His Christ have come, for the accuser of our brethren, who accused them before our God day and night, has been cast down. And they overcame him by the blood of the Lamb and by the word of their testimony, and*

they did not love their lives to the death.

John the Apostle calls the devil the "accuser of the brethren". The Greek word for accuser is "katagoros". It means a complainant at law. So when the Bible speaks of the accuser of the brethren, it is not speaking of someone slandering you in the natural. It is speaking of the devil's activities in the Courts of Heaven. Definitely, people can manifest what is going on in the spiritual, but this idea is something happening in the unseen realm. The accuser is building cases and presenting them before Heaven's court. This is to secure the right to devour and consume if possible. It is to deny us what Jesus paid for that is rightfully ours.

Notice that this accuser is destined to be casted down. We are told it is by the blood of the Lamb, the word of our testimony and not loving our lives unto death. If we are to functionally see the accuser's case against us dismissed, we must employ these three dimensions. We will see how to do this in a later chapter so we can secure the healing that already belongs to us.

Let's look at the three main things the devil uses to build cases against us to stop our healings. They are sin, transgression, and iniquity. We have seen how these three things contributed to David's body being weakened and afflicted.

Sin is the Hebrew word "chataah" and it means an offense. It comes from the word "chet" which means a crime and its penalty. It carries a legal connotation. Sin is a legal issue. It grants the devil legal ground to work against us. Again, this is why we are admonished by Peter to guard against granting the devil legal rights to use against us. First Peter chapter 5 and verse 8 tells us this can allow us to be devoured.

> *Be sober, be vigilant; because your adversary the devil walks about*

like a roaring lion, seeking whom
he may devour.

From his legal place in the spirit, the devil
is building cases against us to devour us. This
word "devour" is the Greek word "katapino"
and it means to gulp down entirely. It also
means to drown. He cannot devour at will.
He has to discover a legal right to do so. One
of the main things the devil uses is sickness
and disease to devour, gulp down, and consume. Sin or anything that is an offense to
God grants our legal opponent this right.
Peter said we must be sober and vigilant not
to give him this right!

There are those who would tell us that the
devil has lost ALL his legal rights because
of the New Covenant established by Jesus.
They would even go so far as to say that I do
not realize what grace has done. They would
accuse me of putting people back under
bondage and even the law by talking about
sin, transgression, and iniquity. Yet I would

point out that none other than Peter seemed to understand what was happening in the spirit realm. Please realize that Peter is a New Testament apostle. He clearly understood that satan is still operating legally against us. This is why he is telling us to be sober and vigilant. We must not give the devil the legal rights are he will use them against us in the Courts of Heaven. If we have given him rights, we must have them revoked so everything Jesus died for us to have can be ours.

Sin can be connected to the motive or intention of the heart. Jesus understood this when He spoke in Matthew chapter 5 and verses 21 through 22 about murder and anger.

> *"You have heard that it was said to those of old, 'You shall not murder, and whoever murders will be in danger of the judgment.' But I say to you that whoever is angry with his brother without a cause shall*

> *be in danger of the judgment. And*
> *whoever says to his brother, 'Raca!'*
> *shall be in danger of the council.*
> *But whoever says, 'You fool!' shall*
> *be in danger of hell fire.*

Jesus said that the state of the heart can be more important than the activity. We must guard our hearts. Notice that Jesus said the words spoken from a bitter, angry, and hateful heart can cause legal troubles in the spirit. Anger without a cause can put us in danger of judgment. This is the Greek word "krisis" and it means a decision from a tribunal for or against. Perhaps we have thought of this just being in the hereafter. What if this occurs in the spirit realm now? What if our words of anger cause judgments to be rendered against us that grants the devil the right to devour? We must repent so these rights are revoked. Could it be that we are not being healed because we will not deal with our hearts and bitterness? There is a judgment against us in the spirit realm that will not allow everything

Jesus died for to manifest in our life. Please, Lord help us!

As Jesus continued speaking, He said if we say "Raca" or "you are worthless", we can be in danger of the council. This word in the Greek is "sunedrion" and it was used to refer to the Jewish Sanhedrin. It meant a joint council or a subordinate tribunal. It was a place where legal decisions were made. Again could it be that Jesus was not just cautioning about the eternal judgment, but also about what is currently happening in the legal dimension of the spirit? Could it be that Jesus was saying there is a "council" in Heaven where verdicts are being rendered based on the state of our heart and the words that flow from it? Have our words of ridicule, and judgment against others allowed legal things against us to hold us in sickness? Again, we must repent. The last thing Jesus addressed were those who label someone as a "fool". Jesus says these can be in danger of the eternal punishment of hell. It would appear

that the first two were about what can happen to us because of legal rights of the devil
to prosecute us. Then Jesus says, ultimately
hell can be the final legal rendering against
us. The motive of our hearts and the words
that flow from it are very important.

We see this in the life of Job. As I shared in
my other books on "The Courts of Heaven"
Job went into terrible situations because the
devil brought an accusation against him.
The accusation is found in Job chapter 1 and
verses 8 through 12.

> *Then the Lord said to Satan,
> "Have you considered My servant
> Job, that there is none like him on
> the earth, a blameless and upright
> man, one who fears God and shuns
> evil?"*
>
> *So Satan answered the Lord and
> said, "Does Job fear God for noth-
> ing? Have You not made a hedge
> around him, around his household,*

and around all that he has on every side? You have blessed the work of his hands, and his possessions have increased in the land. But now, stretch out Your hand and touch all that he has, and he will surely curse You to Your face!"

And the Lord said to Satan, "Behold, all that he has is in your power; only do not lay a hand on his person."

So Satan went out from the presence of the Lord.

The accusation of satan against Job was about the motive and intention of heart. He accused Job of only serving God because of what he could get out of it. The result was devastating things that Job walked through. The case satan brought against Job allowed him to do him massive harm. Part of this was sickness and disease. Job chapter 2 and verses 6 through 8 tells us that severe boils came on Job's body.

*And the Lord said to Satan,
"Behold, he is in your hand, but
spare his life."*
*So Satan went out from the pres-
ence of the Lord, and struck Job
with painful boils from the sole of
his foot to the crown of his head.
And he took for himself a potsherd
with which to scrape himself while
he sat in the midst of the ashes.*

Based on the case satan brought against
Job, the Lord rendered a judgment. Satan
could afflict him with disease and sickness
but could not take his life. Job's sickness
was a result of a legal case satan had against
him. The rest of the book of Job is about this
case being answered. Not only does Job get
healed, but restoration comes to him two-
fold. (Job 42:10)

It is quite interesting that James in James
chapter 5 and verses 9-11 speaks from a New
Testament perspective about what happened

to Job. He connects Job to God as Judge and the Courts of Heaven.

> *Do not grumble against one another, brethren, lest you be condemned. Behold, the Judge is standing at the door! My brethren, take the prophets, who spoke in the name of the Lord, as an example of suffering and patience. Indeed we count them blessed who endure. You have heard of the perseverance of Job and seen the end intended by the Lord—that the Lord is very compassionate and merciful.*

James exhorts about not grumbling and speaking evil of others. His admonishment is the Judge is at the door. I take this to mean, He is listening and discerning and judging. Job's response in the Courts was he received compassion and mercy from the Lord. Healing was secured as well as restoration of wealth and prosperity. We must learn to deal with any motive, wound, hurt, or intention that can be used against us in the Courts of Heaven. Our healing could hang in the balance.

The second thing satan uses to build a case is transgression. Transgression is the Hebrew word "pasha". It is the means a revolt or rebellion. Transgression comes from a word meaning to break away from authority. We transgress when we throw off restraints and say, "We don't care what God thinks, we will do this anyway". It's not just about the activity, but the attitude attached to it. When the devil finds these kinds of things in our lives, he is able to put together a case against us in the Courts of Heaven.

In regards to sickness, we can see this in the story of the man at the Pool of Bethesda in John chapter 5. In this story, we find a man who is waiting for the stirring of the waters in this pool. It is said that when the waters stir whoever gets into them first will be made whole. The Scripture says there was a "great multitude" of sick people around this pool. (Vs. 3) This speaks of the desperation of people to be made well. Yet only the first one in the water on a yearly basis was healed. They attributed the stirring of the water to "an angel". This seems a very cruel scenario. Only one in the midst of a multitude would get healed. This "angel" that is said to stir the waters some have said could have been a "water god". In other words, it was a demonic entity designed to get attention and worship (because this is what they desire, Matthew 4:8) and to distract from who God really is. In the midst of this, Jesus comes to a man with a sickness of thirty-eight years. Jesus asked this man if he wants to be healed? The obvious answer would be yes, wouldn't it? Why would Jesus ask this? The answer is if you have been in condition for thirty-eight years there is a strong possibility your identity is now in your sickness. In other words, you wouldn't know who you were without your sickness. It seems crazy, but people can begin to have emotional connections to their condition. It's what they talk about, think about, maintenance and even live for. These people cannot be healed. This attitude actually can give the devil the legal right to hold them in their sickness.

Once Jesus affirms this man desires healing, He speaks the word, the man responds and is healed. Later Jesus finds the man in John chapter 5 and verse 14 and reveals why this man was sick in the first place.

> *Afterward Jesus found him in the temple, and said to him, "See, you have been made well. Sin no more, lest a worse thing come upon you."*

Jesus clearly says the man's disease was a result of some place of sin in his life. Jesus admonishes him to "sin no more" are something even worse would come on him. His initial condition was a result of the devil having the legal right to afflict him. If he went back to his sin, it would give the devil a legal right to bring something even worse. Matthew chapter 12 and verses 43 through 45 shows us the nature of the demonic.

> *"When an unclean spirit goes out of a man, he goes through dry places, seeking rest, and finds none. Then he says, 'I will return to my house from which I came.' And when he comes, he finds it empty, swept, and put in order. Then he goes and takes with him seven other spirits more wicked than himself, and they enter and dwell there; and the last state of that man is worse than the first. So shall it also be with this wicked generation."*

When the devil's power is broken, he will come back and see if a legal right is being granted to reenter. If it is, he and seven more wicked spirits will come back to torment and afflict. This is what Jesus is warning this man about. It is possible to get healed, but to "lose" your healing because legal rights are granted to the devil. We want to maintain everything the Lord has graciously given us.

I don't know what is worse than thirty-eight years of suffering, but something is. Remember, this man couldn't even get himself in the water. So whatever his condition was, it incapacitated him on some level. Jesus lets us know this particular malady was joined to sin and transgression giving the devil the legal right. We must repent of anything that is in rebellion against God. When I choose to do what I want to do regardless of what God desires, I am granting satan evidence to build legal cases against me. The purpose of the devil's temptation is to gain evidence against us in the Courts of Heaven. In Matthew chapter 4 and verse 3 we see satan tempting Jesus.

> *Now when the tempter came to Him, he said, "If You are the Son of God, command that these stones become bread."*

The purpose of his temptation was to be able to accuse Jesus in the Courts of Heaven and deny Him the right to be our Savior. This is the way the devil works. He tempts us, gets us to fall and then uses it legally against us. This is why Peter so encouraged us to be on guard. Remember again First Peter chapter 5 and verse 8.

> *Be sober, be vigilant; because your adversary the devil walks about like a roaring lion, seeking whom he may devour.*

We are to protect ourselves from the devil as the adversary, our legal opponent, developing legal rights to devour. We must not sin, but if we do, we must repent quickly of every rebellion that allowed this activity. Otherwise the devil can use this to bring sickness and disease against us.

The other word used to build legal cases against us to afflict with disease is iniquity. It is the Hebrew word "avon". It means perversity. It comes from a word meaning to be crooked. This word is associated with the sins in our heritage. Jeremiah chapter 14 and verse 20 shows a repentance of personal sins and the iniquities of the fathers.

> *We acknowledge, O Lord, our wickedness*
> *And the iniquity of our fathers,*
> *For we have sinned against You.*

It is the iniquity of the fathers that causes a crooked and even twisting of our desires and longings. Iniquities can twist our very nature. We feel pulls of temptation based on what our fathers have allowed. It gives the devil the legal right to work against us.

This must have been a common thought in the times of Jesus. The disciples bring it up as a reason why a man was born in a certain condition. John chapter 9 and verses 1 through 7 chronicles the healing of a blind man.

Now as Jesus passed by, He saw a man who was blind from birth. And His disciples asked Him, saying, "Rabbi, who sinned, this man or his parents, that he was born blind?"

Jesus answered, "Neither this man nor his parents sinned, but that the works of God should be revealed in him. I must work the works of Him who sent Me while it is day; the night is coming when no one can work. As long as I am in the world, I am the light of the world." When He had said these things, He spat on the ground and made clay with the saliva; and He anointed the eyes of the blind man with the clay. And He said to him, "Go, wash in the pool of Siloam" (which is translated, Sent). *So he went and washed, and came back seeing.*

The disciples felt it was some kind of sin in this man's history that allowed him to be born unable to see. Jesus said in this situation that isn't the case. Many people take this one occasion to mean that the sins of previous generations cannot cause sickness in a person. I've never thought this was what Jesus was saying. I've understood that Jesus was referring to this individual circumstance. He was saying, "In this case, it wasn't generational issues that caused the blindness". Yet the possibility does exist that the iniquity in a person's ancestry can give the devil legal right to bring such things into being. We must be discerning when dealing with sickness and disease. This is so very true, when people are seeking sincerely, yet are not being healed. Searching out the legal issue the devil is using to hold someone in a place of affliction can be essential to that person being healed. This is what I now understand the Lord meant when He said to my wife Mary, "You must pray for them correctly or they will die".

In the chapters to come, we will examine some issues in our bloodline that satan can legally use to hold us in a place of sickness. If we can discern his case against us, we can then revoke it by the blood of Jesus in The Courts of Heaven. Once this occurs, the devil no longer has a legal right to keep us in this place. We are free to receive fully everything Jesus died for us to have.

In the next chapter, we will see the legal work of Jesus on the cross and the verdict that has resulted. This is absolutely necessary to recognize what we are now doing in the Courts of Heaven. Get ready, healing is close, even at hand! Here is a prayer to begin to be positioned in His Courts.

> *"Lord, thank You for the third dimension of prayer of coming before You as Judge. Lord, I ask for Your help to stand before You in the Court system of Heaven and present my case. I thank You that*

You help me take everything You have done and present it before Your Courts. As I do, let every accusation against me be removed and allow healing to flow into our lives. In Jesus, Name, amen."

ABOUT ROBERT HENDERSON

Robert Henderson is a global apostolic leader who operates in revelation and impartation. His teaching empowers the Body of Christ to see the hidden truths of Scripture clearly and apply them for breakthrough results. Driven by a mandate to disciple nations through writing and speaking, Robert travels extensively around the globe, teaching on the apostolic, the Kingdom of God, the "Seven Mountains," and most notably the Courts of Heaven. He has been married to Mary for over 40 years. They have six children and five grandchildren. Together they are enjoying life in beautiful Midlothian, Texas.